Weekly Reader Books presents

# Mine and Yours

A Children's Book about Rights and Responsibilities

by

## Joy Wilt

Illustrated by Ernie Hergenroeder

Educational Products Division
Word, Incorporated
Waco, Texas

# Author

JOY WILT is creator and director of Children's Ministries, an organization that provides resources "for people who care about children"—speakers, workshops, demonstrations, consulting services, and training institutes. A certified elementary school teacher, administrator, and early childhood specialist, Joy is also consultant to and professor in the master's degree program in children's ministries for Fuller Theological Seminary. Joy is a graduate of LaVerne College, LaVerne, California (B.A. in Biological Science), and Pacific Oaks College, Pasadena, California (M.A. in Human Development). She is author of three books, *Happily Ever After, An Uncomplicated Guide to Becoming a Superparent,* and *Taming the Big Bad Wolves,* as well as the popular *Can-Make-And-Do Books.* Joy's commitment "never to forget what it feels like to be a child" permeates the many innovative programs she has developed and her work as lecturer, consultant, writer, and—not least—mother of two children, Christopher and Lisa.

# Artist

ERNIE HERGENROEDER is founder and owner of Hergie & Associates (a visual communications studio and advertising agency). With the establishment of this company in 1975, "Hergie" and his wife, Faith, settled in San Jose with their four children, Lynn, Kathy, Stephen, and Beth. Active in community and church affairs, Hergie is involved in presenting creative workshops for teachers, ministers, and others who wish to understand the techniques of communicating visually. He also lectures in high schools to encourage young artists toward a career in commercial art. Hergie serves as a consultant to organizations such as the Police Athletic League (PAL), Girl Scouts, and religious and secular corporations. His ultimate goal is to touch the hearts of kids (8 to 80) all over the world—visually!

This book is a presentation of Weekly Reader Books.
Weekly Reader Books offers book clubs for children from
preschool through junior high school.

For further information write to:
WEEKLY READER BOOKS
1250 Fairwood Ave.
Columbus, Ohio 43216

Mine and Yours

# Contents

# Introduction

<u>Mine and Yours</u> is one of a series of books. The complete set is called ***Ready-Set-Grow!***

<u>Mine and Yours</u> deals with human rights and responsibilities and can be used by itself or as a part of a program that utilizes all of the ***Ready-Set-Grow!*** books.

<u>Mine and Yours</u> is specifically designed for children four to eight years of age. A child can either read the book or have it read to him or her. This can be done at home, church, or school.

<u>Mine and Yours</u> is designed to involve the child in the concepts that are being taught. This is done by simply and carefully explaining each concept and then asking questions that invite a response from the child. It is hoped that by answering the questions the child will personalize the concept and, thus, integrate it into his or her thinking.

Mine and Yours teaches that just as a person is born with a body, a mind, and a soul, a person is born with rights — rights that should be retained and asserted if the person is to survive and grow. Rights are not something that a person receives from other people. Rights are something a person automatically owns.

One interpretation of "love your neighbor as yourself" can be "allow others to retain and assert their rights as you retain and assert your rights."

Mine and Yours is designed to teach children that they have rights just as every other person does. It also teaches that with every right there is a corresponding responsibility.

Only after children are taught what their rights are can they retain and assert them, and only after children are taught what their responsibilities are can they assume them.

You have
human rights
and responsibilities.

A right is a privilege you are entitled to.

A responsibility is something you are supposed to do.

Because you are a human being, you automatically have certain rights and responsibilities.

You own your rights just as you own your body,
your feelings, and your thoughts.

Your rights
belong to you,
and no one is entitled
to take them away.

13

This book will tell you what rights you have as a human being.

It will also tell you about your human responsibilities.

# Right No. 1

## The Right to Be Yourself

This is Joanne.

Joanne's parents wish that in some ways she were different.

17

Joanne's brother Eugene wishes that in some ways she were different.

Joanne's grandparents wish that
in some ways
she were different.

19

Joanne's friend Diane wishes that in some ways she were different.

Joanne's teacher wishes that in some ways she were different.

But Joanne cannot be everything her parents, brother, grandparents, friends and teacher want her to be. Joanne can only be herself.

All these things:

> what Joanne likes,
> what Joanne is interested in,
> what Joanne thinks,
> what makes Joanne laugh,
> how Joanne shows her feelings,
> how Joanne feels and acts around people,
> what Joanne is good and not good at doing,
> what Joanne's good and bad habits are,
> whether or not Joanne does what she says she will do,
> whether Joanne is a hard worker or lazy,
> whether Joanne is neat or messy, and
> whether Joanne does things quickly or slowly

. . . make Joanne the person that she is.

Joanne has the right to be her own person, and so do you!

# Right No. 2

## The Right to Be Honest

This is Kevin.

Sometimes Kevin is forced to say "I'm sorry" when he really isn't sorry. **27**

**Sometimes Kevin is forced to say "thank you" when he really isn't thankful.**

28

Sometimes Kevin is forced to say "yes" when
he would really like to say "no."

29

Sometimes Kevin is forced to say that he doesn't mind when he really does mind, or that things are OK when they really aren't.

Sometimes Kevin is forced to say he understands when he really doesn't understand.

Sometimes Kevin is forced to say that he is not feeling a certain way when he really is.

Sometimes Kevin is forced to say that he agrees when he really doesn't agree.

THERE! NOW THAT I'VE EXPLAINED WHY YOU CAN'T SPEND THE NIGHT AT STEVE'S HOUSE, I'M SURE YOU AGREE THAT IT'S THE BEST THING FOR EVERYONE.

Kevin needs to be thoughtful and kind, but Kevin also
needs to be honest.
Here are some kind, and yet honest, things that Kevin
could possibly say.

<u>To his little brother</u> —"It probably wasn't right for me to
hit you, but I was very angry and upset with you for breaking
my toy.  Please don't get into my things again."

<u>To his grandmother</u> —"It was very kind of you to get me this
suit.  I appreciate what you did.  Thank you for thinking about
me."

<u>To the dinner hostess</u> — "No, thank you!  I would not care for
any spinach."

34

<u>To his mother</u> —"But I do mind someone playing with my toys without asking me first. It is not  OK  to get into my things without my permission."

<u>To his teacher</u> —"I'm sure this problem is simple to you and others, but I do not understand how to do it. Please help me."

<u>To the nurse</u> —"I am very nervous about getting shots. They scare me. Please try to understand."

<u>To his father</u> —"Thank you for explaining to me why I can't go to Steve's house. I understand how you feel now, and I won't go to Steve's, but I don't agree with you that it is the best thing for everyone."

Kevin has the right to be honest, and so do you!

# Right No. 3

## The Right to Have Your Needs Met

This is Lillian.

Lillian has a body that needs air, food, water, exercise, and rest.

Lillian needs to have other people love her.

She needs others to value  and care for her.

Lillian also needs
to love others.

40

Lillian needs to have other people respect her. She needs others to admire her and think good things about her.

I LIKE YOU JUST THE WAY YOU ARE.

Lillian also needs to respect others.

Lillian needs to have others trust her. She needs others to know that she is honest and fair.

THANK YOU FOR GETTING MY GROCERIES AND BRINGING BACK MY CHANGE. I KNEW I COULD TRUST YOU.

Lillian also needs to trust others.

42

Lillian needs to feel secure.
She needs to know what to expect from others.

43

Lillian needs to be creative.  She needs to make things and do things that have not been done before.

Lillian needs to think and learn. She needs to be curious, explore, and discover things.

Without hurting herself or anyone else, Lillian has the right to:

see that her body gets plenty of air, food, water, exercise, and rest;

make friends and develop relationships with people who will love, respect, and trust her; and

make friends and develop relationships with people that she can love, respect, and trust.

Without hurting herself or anyone else, Lillian has the right to be creative. She has the right to make things and do things that have not been done before. Lillian has the right to think and learn. She has the right to be curious, explore, and discover things.

Lillian has the right to have her needs met, and so do you!

# Right No. 4

## The Right to Ask Questions and Get Honest Answers, and the Right to Learn

This is Denton.

There are many things Denton would like to know about.

There are many questions he would like to ask.

50

But sometimes Denton asks people questions, and they are too busy to give him answers.

Sometimes Denton asks people questions, and they
tell him that his questions are not important.

Sometimes Denton asks people questions, and they tell him that he is too young to understand.

Sometimes Denton asks people questions, and they tell him that he does not need to know the answers.

Sometimes Denton asks people questions,
and they do not know the answers.

Denton must ask questions and get honest answers if he is to learn and grow. He should never stop asking questions. Here are some things Denton could possibly say when people do not give him good answers to his questions:

A good response to "I'm too busy now to answer your question" is "I see that you are busy, so I will not bother you. But before I leave, would you tell me <u>when</u> you will be able to answer my question?"

A good response to "Your question is not important" is "My question may not be important to you, but it is to me. That is why I asked it. Could you please give me an answer?"

A good response to "You're too young to understand" is "If I am old enough to ask the question, I feel that I am old enough to understand the answer. Please answer my question."

A good response to "You don't need to know the answer" is "Yes, I do. I need to know about the things that make me curious. I want to understand the things that I do not know about. Please answer my question."

A good response to "I don't know the answer to your question" is "If you do not know the answer to my question, can you tell me where I can go or what I can do to find the answer myself?"

If a person says, "I do not want to answer your question," a good response is "If you do not want to answer my question, do you know someone else I could ask?"

Denton has the right to ask questions and get honest answers.
Denton has the right to learn, and so do you!

# Right No. 5

## The Right to Think Your Own Thoughts
## and Believe Your Own Beliefs

This is Peter.

Peter is interested in outer space. He believes that there are living things on other planets in the universe.

Peter believes that there are many other worlds
in the universe just like our world.

Peter's friends do not agree with him. They do not believe that there are living things on other planets or that there are other worlds in the universe.

63

Peter thinks that monster movies are great!

Peter's sister Mary does not agree.

She would rather watch sad, romantic movies.

Peter's parents think that he would make a fine concert pianist when he grows up.

Peter does not agree with his parents about becoming a concert pianist. He thinks he would be better as a scientist.

Although his family and friends do not always agree with him, Peter has the right to think his own thoughts and believe his own beliefs.

Peter has the right to:

> like whatever he chooses to like,
> be interested in whatever interests him,
> believe what he chooses to believe,
> think what he chooses to think, and
> feel how he really feels.

Peter has the right to think his own thoughts and believe his own beliefs,

and so do you!

70

# Right No. 6

## The Right to Make Mistakes

**This is Carrie.**

**Sometimes Carrie has accidents.**

Sometimes Carrie makes wrong choices.

**Sometimes Carrie makes mistakes.**

Carrie, along with every other person in the world, has accidents and makes wrong choices and mistakes. Accidents, wrong choices, and mistakes are an important part of life. Although they are embarrassing and sometimes cause pain, they can help people learn and grow.

When Carrie has an accident, she learns to be more careful.

When Carrie makes a wrong choice, she learns to ask questions, get help from other people, and think more carefully before she makes choices.

When Carrie makes a mistake, she learns more about herself and how she can live her life better.

Carrie has the right to make mistakes, and so do you!

# Right No. 7

## The Right to Make All the Decisions and Choices You Can, and the Right to Be in on Any Decision That Will Affect You

This is Marvin.

Sometimes people say that Marvin will do something without asking him first.

Sometimes people do things that will affect Marvin without asking him first.

84

Marvin has the right to contribute (give) to decisions that will affect him.

Here are some kind, and yet honest, things Marvin could possibly say.

To his mother — "Mother, it was kind of you to buy me this suit. However, I do not like it and would not feel comfortable wearing it. So that we don't waste your money, could we return this suit and pick out one that we could both agree on?"

To his father — "Father, it was kind of you to take the time to sign me up for Little League, but I do not want to play baseball. Is there a possibility that I could be on the swimming team instead?"

To his grandmother — "I do not want to embarrass you, so I will mow your neighbor's lawn this time. But please, Grandmother, ask me before you tell anyone that I will do something. I would like to talk it over with you before you volunteer me."

<u>To his friend Bill</u> (sometime when Aaron is not around) — "I was looking forward to playing chess with you.  When you brought Aaron, I was disappointed because we weren't able to play chess.  Please let me know before you change any plans that we make together."

<u>To his teacher</u> — "I am glad that you liked my story.  I am honored that you thought it was good enough to print in the school newspaper.  However, the story is personal; and if it is not too late, I would appreciate it if you would get it back before it is printed."

Marvin has the right to make any choices or
decisions that he can. He also has the right to
be in on any decision that will affect him, and
so do you!

# Right No. 8

## The Right to Own Your Own Things

This is Laura.

Laura received a watch, a purse, and
two books for her birthday. Now Laura
owns the watch, the purse, and the books.

Laura received a bike, a doll, and two record albums for Christmas. Now Laura owns the bike, the doll, and the record albums.

Laura saved her allowance and worked at odd
jobs until she had enough money to buy some
roller skates. She bought the skates with her
own money, and now she owns them.

Laura found a hungry, stray cat on her front porch one morning. Her parents tried to find its owner, but when they couldn't, they said that Laura could keep the cat. Now Laura owns it.

Laura traded her jump rope for a baseball.
Now Laura owns the baseball.

The things Laura owns belong to her.  As long as she does not hurt herself or anyone else, she can do whatever she wants to do with her things.

> She can insist that no one else use them, or she can share them.
> She can use her things, or she can save them.

It is true that Laura can destroy the things she owns, but this is <u>never</u> a wise thing to do.

If she does not want a certain thing anymore, she should:

> put it away and save it as a memento from her childhood,
> give it to someone who wants or needs it,
> trade it for something that she wants, or
> sell it.

The things Laura owns belong to her. Therefore, they are her responsibility. If she wants to keep her things, she needs to avoid losing, misusing, damaging, or destroying them. She also needs to make sure that no one else loses, misuses, damages, or destroys them. She can do this by:

> putting her things away when they are not being used  and by not loaning them to people who may abuse them.

Laura has the right to own her own things, and so do you!

# Right No. 9

# The Right to Privacy

This is Jamie.

Although Jamie likes to be with people most of the time, once in a while he likes to be alone.

Most of the time Jamie
doesn't mind telling other
people how he feels, but
sometimes he'd rather
not say.

102

Jamie needs to be alone sometimes so that he can think and daydream or do things without being distracted or disturbed.  It's OK for Jamie to get away from people for a while and be alone, as long as he tells someone where he will be.  This is so that people will not think that he is lost and worry about him.

Jamie does not have to tell everyone how he's feeling all the time. It's OK for Jamie to have private feelings.  Jamie does not have to tell everyone what he is thinking all the time.  It's OK for Jamie to have private thoughts.

**Jamie has the right to privacy, and so do you!**

# Right No. 10

## The Right to Live Free from Fear

This is Harold.

Harold has to walk to school every day. Although Harold wishes he didn't have to, he takes the long way to school because he's afraid that if he goes the short way . . .

he would see Thad (the school bully).

Harold is afraid that Thad will beat him up.

Harold has heard from the kids at school that the principal has a huge paddle that he spanks students with if they ever do anything wrong.

Harold lives in fear of being spanked by the principal.

Harold has heard that a mean old man and a mean old lady who hate children live in the old, run-down house close to where Harold lives.

Harold does not walk by their house because he is afraid that they might see him and hurt him.

It is not good for Harold to be afraid all the time.

It is not good for any person to be afraid all the time.

People who are afraid all the time need to get help.

Sometimes understanding or knowing about the things that a person fears will help the person get over being afraid. If Harold does not want to be afraid all the time, he needs to have someone help him deal with Thad. He should also find out if the stories about the principal are true. If they are, Harold should find out <u>exactly</u> what entitles a person to a spanking, avoid doing those things, and then <u>know</u> that he will never get a spanking. Last, Harold needs to find out the truth about the old lady and old man and then decide what to do about it.

Harold must do something about his fears.

Harold has the right to live   free from fear, and so do you!

# Right No. 11

## The Right to Grow and Develop at Your Own Pace

This is Lucy.

Sometimes Lucy's family wishes that she were older and could do more things on her own.

Sometimes Lucy's friends wish that she were older and could do more things.

Although it may be easier on everyone else for Lucy to be able to think and act like a grown-up person, Lucy is only four years old. Because Lucy is four, she thinks and acts like a four-year-old. This is the way it should be. People should not have to think or act older or younger than their age. People have a right to grow and develop as they are able—at their own pace.

Lucy has the right to grow and develop at her own pace, and so do you!

# Right No. 12

## The Right to Defend Your Rights if They Are Being Taken Away

You have the right to:

> be your own person,
>
> be honest,
>
> get your needs met,
>
> ask questions and obtain honest answers,
>
> think your own thoughts and believe your own beliefs,
>
> make mistakes,
>
> make the decisions and choices that you can, and be in on the decisions that will affect you,
>
> own your own things,
>
> have privacy,
>
> live free from fear, and
>
> grow and develop at your own pace.

But remember, rights demand responsibilities. For every right there is a corresponding responsibility.

# WHAT DOES THAT MEAN?

If you want to be your own person,
you have the <u>responsibility</u> to allow other people to be their
own persons.

If you want to be honest,
you have the <u>responsibility</u> to allow other people to be honest.

If you want to get your needs met,
you have the <u>responsibility</u> of allowing other people to get
their needs met.

If you want to ask questions and get honest answers,
you have the <u>responsibility</u> of allowing other people to ask
questions and get honest answers.

If you want to think your own thoughts and believe your own beliefs,
you have the <u>responsibility</u> of allowing other people to think
their own thoughts and believe their own beliefs.

If you want to make mistakes,
you have the responsibility of allowing other people to make mistakes.

If you want to make choices and decisions, and be in on the decisions that affect you,
you have the responsibility of allowing other people to make choices and decisions, and be in on the decisions that affect them.

If you want to own your own things,
you have the responsibility of allowing other people to own their own things.

If you want to have privacy,
you have the responsibility of allowing other people to have privacy.

If you want to live a life free from fear,
you have the responsibility of allowing other people to live lives free from fear.

If you want to grow and develop at your own pace,
you have the responsibility of allowing other people to grow and develop at their own paces.

Human rights are

something to which every human being is entitled.

Because this is true, there is a Right No. 12:


The Right to Defend Your Rights if They Are Being Taken Away

This means that you should not allow anyone to take your rights away.  You need to keep them, be thankful for them, and use them wisely because . . .

Your rights and responsibilities were given to you
so that you could become the wonderful person you were created to be!